Him Only:

A Servant's Walk with the Lord

Shelia Gaines

Mossy Creek PRESS

CARSON-NEWMAN COLLEGE

Him Only:

A Servant's Walk with the Lord

Shelia Gaines

Mossy Creek Press

Copyright (C) 2011 by Shelia Gaines

ISBN: 978-1-936912-34-6   Softcover

This book was printed in the United States of America.

To order additional copies of this book, contact:
Mossy Creek Press
1-423-475-7308
www.mossycreekpress.com

Table of Contents

Introduction

Then said Jesus unto him, Get thee hence,
Satan: for it is written, Thou shalt worship
the Lord thy God, and him only shall thou
serve. Matthew 4:10

EMPLOYEES AT WALMART WEAR A VEST with the question "How may I serve you?" on the back. As far as I know, they have worn them for years and many people probably don't pay any attention to the question. The very nature of the question implies a willingness to help whenever and wherever needed. I suspect the store's management wants to let the customers know how important they are to WalMart and to emphasize the fact that the employee's number one goal is to serve the customer.

Undoubtedly more than one employee of WalMart has had to serve an unhappy customer at one time or another. However, the attitude of the customer is not supposed to change the attitude of the employee, nor affect the quality of the service.

Although admittedly not a common comparison to serving God, that question on the WalMart work vest

7

makes me think of different ways to serve. Some people serve in the armed forces and some people serve in public service such as restaurants or retail. Service encompasses a vast array of occupations in all arenas, both secular and religious.

In the community where I grew up, signs in many of the churches read, "Enter and Worship, Depart and Serve." I haven't seen many of these signs in a long time, but I remember them still and I wonder how others perceived them.

I actually never thought of what it meant until recent years. Many people naturally equate going to church with serving God. Hopefully, the majority of those people also realize that corporate worship is only a very small part of our service to God. "Depart and serve" suggests to me that our service happens or at least continues after we leave the church building. In order to truly serve God, our daily life outside the walls of the church must reflect how we worship or serve in the church. Our desire to serve him must match our desire to walk with him.

Not everyone will serve the Lord from the pulpit as pastors. However, as Christians, we all have a responsibility to serve God. How we serve him, the length to which we are willing to go and the sacrifices we are willing to make in our walk of faith depends on our level of commitment to him. That commitment requires serving God at all costs and continuing the walk of faith.

I heard gospel artist and pastor, Donnie McClurkin, comment that the church used to be called the church house. He suggested that the more modern version of the church fails to allow people to remember that the church building is nothing more than the physical structure that houses the people of God when they come together for corporate worship. The real church should be within us.

Service awards are given all the time in businesses and organizations. Sometimes it is a merit reward for a job well done and other times it is for loyalty to the company for so many years. Some people stay with the same company for many years because they enjoy working there or because of the salary and benefits. There was a time when you could expect to stay with the same company for the duration of your career if you wanted to. This does not happen much anymore because many companies now change hands often. Many people today are more mobile and do not expect to, or even wish to, remain at the same company for a lifetime of employment.

As America's attitude toward the workplace becomes more relaxed, we run the risk of our attitude toward the quality of work suffering also. In a similar fashion, as more churches begin to "relax" the formality of their services, they risk the second part of the verse in John 8:11, "neither do I condemn thee, go and sin no more." In an effort to be more inclusive, many churches are not fulfilling their responsibility to the very people they are accountable to. It requires a delicate balance to maintain the integrity of our walk with the Lord without isolating the people we need to bring into the kingdom.

Psalms 37:23-24 reminds us that "the steps of a good man are ordered by the Lord: and he delighteth in his way. Though he fall, he shall not be utterly cast down: for the Lord upholdeth him with his hand." You cannot expect God to order your steps if you are afraid to begin the walk.

It has been said that walking is one of the best forms of physical exercise. It is a simple exercise with enormous benefits. Walking just twenty minutes a day can improve your health. Just as physical walking is easy and beneficial to your health, a spiritual walk with the Lord is beneficial to your soul. This book examines our walk with the Lord by comparing it to physical exercise, specifically walking.

Intentional exercise is very important today because of the nature of our lifestyles. Once, most people worked hard at physical labor simply to survive. Now, even agricultural professions have more advanced machinery that requires less manpower. While this has helped to make some jobs less physically taxing, it has also led to more obesity. American children now spend more time on the computer and less time doing physical exercise, prompting changes to school lunch programs by the FDA. The news media is full of stories about the pitfalls of a nation that does not take care of itself physically. There is an emotional and financial price to pay for neglecting one's health in an effort to be more prosperous.

The message seems to be "get up and get moving." This is evidenced by the creation of benefit walks for many worthy causes (cancer, Alzheimer's, diabetes, etc.). The call to become spiritually fit has mirrored this movement.

"Walking with the Lord" is a term used loosely these days. I have recently begun to examine exactly what that phrase implies. In Amos 3:3, the Bible asks how two can walk together except they agree. I would submit the question, if we do not agree with the Lord on how we should walk our Christian walk, are we truly walking with him? Is it possible to walk with the Lord without serving him? I don't believe we can. That is one of the reasons I refer to our Christian walk as a servant walk. I use the term servant walk because if we walk in the love of God by faith, we walk to serve him. If we truly allow him to order our steps, then we are not afraid to serve him whole-heartedly.

In the second verse of III John, we find these words: "I wish above all that you would prosper and be in good health even as your soul prospers." This advice was given hundreds of years before health and fitness experts began to preach the advantages of healthy living and exercise on our overall health. If our walk with the Lord is to be beneficial to our spiritual health, then we must couple our desire to serve the Lord with our willingness to follow him.

This reminds me of a song called "I have decided to follow Jesus." There is a line, "no turning back, no, no, no turning back." Sometimes we start out with the intent of walking a certain number of miles but unforeseen circumstances cause us to turn back. When we make a commitment to God, then we need to follow through with it. God is as committed to helping us finish our course as Satan is to putting obstacles in our path in order to keep us off course.

In the first chapter of the book of Job, Satan asked the Lord if Job was serving him for naught. He believed that if Job lost all his blessings, he would lose his love for the Lord. Satan took on the task of attempting to turn Job's heart away from God. He was not successful. Would God get the same results from you that he did from Job? Think about it. What happens when Satan considers your life as a servant of God? Where are you in your walk? Can God trust you to continue to serve him no matter what? Would he find you truly living the meaning of Matthew 4:10 ...thou shalt worship the Lord thy God and Him only shalt thou serve?

In John 21:16, Jesus asked Peter, "loveth thou me?" He responded to Peter's positive answer with "Feed My Sheep." Serving a God that we cannot see means serving our brothers and sisters. Jesus said he came not to be served, but to serve. He was God himself but he was not above washing the feet of the disciples.

In one of Joyce Myers' sermons, I heard her comment on how some people may be honored to be given an opportunity to serve someone well known but absolutely miss the significance of being a servant to someone in their own family, church or business.

Jesus admonishes the people of this same concept in Matthew 25:41-46:

> *Then shall he say also unto them on the left hand, Depart from me, ye cursed, into everlasting fire, prepared for the devil and his angels. For I was an hungered, and ye gave me no meat; I was thirsty, and ye gave me no drink; I was a stranger, and ye took me not in; naked, and ye clothed me not;*

sick, and in prison, and ye visited me not. Then shall they also answer him, saying Lord, when saw we thee an hungered; or athirst, or a stranger, or naked, or sick, or in prison, and did not minister unto thee? Then shall he answer them saying, Verily I say unto you, Inasmuch as ye did it not to one of the least of these, ye did it not to me. And these shall go away to everlasting punishment; but the righteous into life eternal.

That scripture reiterates Joyce Meyers' point that true service to God requires serving his people. You cannot walk up to God and hand him a glass of water, but you can serve your brothers and sisters here on earth. Consider the following verses from 2 John (6-7), suggesting that our love for the Lord whom we have not seen be evident in the love we show our brothers and sisters we see everyday as we take a closer look at walking with the Lord.

And this is love, that we walk after his commandments. This is the commandment. That, as ye have heard from the beginning, ye should walk in it.

Chapter 1
Beginning the Walk

Stand in the ways and see and ask for
the old paths where the good way is and
walk in it;
then you will find rest for your souls,
but they said we will not walk in it.
Jeremiah 6:16

IN ORDER TO PREPARE MOSES TO LEAD the children of Egypt to the promise land, God required him to make some tough choices. Pharaoh did not allow the children of Israel to simply walk away at Moses' request. Some people may think that it was harsh for the Lord to harden the heart of Pharaoh and not allow the people to be set free the first time. I used to wonder about that myself. Many times during their pilgrimage, the Israelites wished to be back with Pharaoh rather than do what was required to stay where they were. However, God had a plan and it was to come to pass with or without them. He had already prepared Moses for this from birth.

Moses just did not realize it.

I watched an interview with the pilot, Captain Chesley "Sully" Sullenberger, who landed the plane in the Hudson River in December 2008 and was immediately struck by something he said. He had worked for many years as a pilot. He had even trained people how to make emergency landings. Between him and the flight crew were many years of experience. He said that it was as if his whole life had been preparing him for that particular moment. If someone were to ask any of us if we would like to train for a time when over 200 lives would be in our hands and we would have to make a miracle landing on the river, our immediate response would probably be no.

We often mention in our Women's Bible Study the wisdom of God in not allowing us to know what we will have to go through all the time, but allowing us to have faith in him if we will just believe. "If you make one step, God will make two" is a quotation falsely attributed to the Bible. That statement is not in the Bible. However, I suspect the principle behind this quote is biblically consistent. God has told us in his word to come unto him, but he does not force us to come. He has told us what to do to accept him as our Lord and Savior, but it has to be our choice. He told Joshua to open his mouth and he would speak for him. But, it's always up to us to make that first step. When God asked Moses to lead the Israelites out of Egypt, to the assurance came in Exodus 3:12: "And he said, Certainly I will be with thee..." Therefore, I believe that when people say, "if you make one step, God will make two," they refer to the belief that if we step out on faith and put our trust in God, he will lead us to and through each successive step and continue to guide us and keep us on the right path.

Many people never reach their full potential because they allow fear of failure to keep them from making the first step. As an academic librarian, I have seen students spend so much time researching a major paper that they don't allow enough to time to write the paper adequately. They often end up frustrated with the results because they do not follow the recommend timeline of the professor recommends. The extra time that they put into the research at the beginning is seen by them as extra dedication instead of procrastination. When they begin research for the paper, four to six weeks can seem like a long time. Panic does not usually set in until they are on the verge of the deadline for the rough draft and only have a few, if any, pages actually ready for the professor's review. It is at this point they see the reasoning of following the timeline and perhaps the wisdom of I Corinthians 14:40.

When children are born, they need medical checkups more often to ensure they are healthy and are growing at a proper rate. If they are not off to a good start, there will be trouble at a later growth stage. Most children will crawl before they walk. After they crawl, they begin to pull up and take a few unsteady steps before they walk unassisted. It is only natural for them to fall a few times. They just get up and keep going. Pretty soon they are not only walking but running.

The same thing is true in our spiritual walk. It is fine to start off slowly, but our goal should be growing closer to God and developing a more meaningful relationship with him all the time.

When you first begin to walk or exercise, you will not necessarily see immediate results. However, you have to believe that, if you continue the regimen, you will be rewarded with a healthier lifestyle. Our walk with the Lord is to receive eternal life. God has not promised us that the walk will be easy but he did say, "*Take my yoke upon you and learn of me for my yoke is easy and my burden is light*" (Matthew 11:30).

Luke 8:11-15 is an excellent example of how our walk with the Lord should begin. This seed parable lets us know that we have to be "rooted and grounded" as I used to hear many older saints say when I was growing up.

Sometimes you can receive the word with joy, but if you do not allow it to take root in your heart, you will be easily tempted and led astray. Or you can start your journey with good intentions, but allow the cares and troubles of this world to distract you. Only the seed that falls on fertile soil will take root and grow. The fifteenth verse lets us know that the only good ground for the word is an honest and good heart.

In physical exercise, this principle would be seen as core training. The core of our physical body, the center of our body (our abdominal area and all muscles that stabilize the spine and pelvis) is very important. These muscle groups are critical for the transfer of energy from large to small body parts during many sporting activities. (www.sports-fitness -advisor.com). The benefits of core strength training are:

- Greater efficiency of movement

- Improved body control and balance

- Increased power output from both the core
  musculature and peripheral muscles such as the shoulders, arms and legs reduced risk of injury (the core muscles act as shock absorbers for jumps and rebounds etc.)

- Improved balance and stability

- Improved athletic performance

The core of our spiritual body is our heart. So many times we say "God knows my heart." This is a serious statement to make because God really does know. We can treat people a certain way to get them to follow our agenda, but God knows our true intent. He knows if our love is just words or if we truly love someone from the bottom of our heart. Service from the heart to the glory of God differs from giving lip service to those who can further our ministry or our career.

Matthew 12:34 lets us know that out of the abundance of the heart, the mouth speaks. We can fool people for a while, but eventually what is in our heart will come out in our actions if not in our words. I think of David being described as a man after God's own heart. He was far from perfect and he made many mistakes, but his heart was right.

David's walk with the Lord began at an early age when he was chosen as a last resort to fight Goliath. All of the sons of Jesse were considered before him. No one believe he was even worthy of being considered. Yet, he did as a child what other men of war had not been able to do.

When David fought Goliath, they put Saul's armor on him but it was too big. David took it off and took a slingshot and some stones. The people thought it was foolish of him to go up against a giant without what they considered proper armor. David, however, went up with God's armor of faith, righteousness and truth. The whole armor of God is described in Ephesians 6:13 -17:

Wherefore take upon you the whole armor of God, that ye may be able to withstand in the evil day, and having done all, to stand. Stand therefore, having your loins girt about with truth, and having on the breastplate of righteousness; And your feet shod with the preparation of the gospel of peace; Above all, taking the shield of faith, wherewith ye shall be able to quench all the fiery darts of the wicked. And take the helmet of salvation, and the sword of the Spirit, and watching thereunto with all perseverance and supplication for all saints:

Other people thought that he needed physical armor to go up against a giant like Goliath, but David trusted fully in the Lord to deliver him. It looked like he was outmatched. However, God had the battle in control all along. Sometimes we are reluctant to begin a true walk with the Lord because we feel we are unequipped. We fail to realize that if God calls us, he will equip us just as he equipped

David for his fight.

The Marines used to have the slogan, "There are only a few good men. They've been to the Marines." I use that example not to bring attention to the Marines in particular, but to the military in general. The military is all about order and protocol. When you sign up to serve in the military, you sign up to serve their way, whether or not you think their way is the best way. There are few circumstances in which you are allowed to void the contract. You do what you are told to do when and how you are told to do it.

This Christian walk is sometimes referred to as being a soldier for God. When the children of Israel were spying out the land, most of them did not look with their spiritual eyes. All they saw was people who were larger than they were. However, Joshua and Caleb trusted God and said "we are well able to take the land." The people who did not believe caused the rest of the people to have to go around in circles for years while the unbelievers died out (Numbers 13:30-14:35).

If we are going to walk with the Lord, we must walk **with** him and not ahead or behind him.

When the military marches in a formation, everybody moves together. There is a unified front. In the book of Joshua, when he was at the Battle of Jericho, God commanded him to encompass the city with warriors. He told them a certain order. March around the city once every day for six days and on the seventh day march around the city seven times and blow the trumpets. They did exactly as God commanded and took the city. They did not request a meeting to discuss whether or not that was the best strategy. They did not dwell on what was going on inside the city while they were marching around it. Their only concern was doing what God had asked them to do. They shouted the victory even before the walls came down. We can follow their example in our own walk even when we are faced with tough situations. We do not have to wait until the battle is over. We can shout now. It does not matter where we are in the battle. It just matters that we keep allowing the Lord to fight for us because the battle is not ours anyway, it is the Lord's and he has never lost a battle.

In some churches, they sing what is called a congregational song: "I'm a soldier.". The song leader will sing a phrase and the congregation will respond with "in the army of the Lord" the first time and with "in the army" the second time.

Leader:	*I'm a soldier.*
Congregation:	*In the army of the Lord.*
Leader:	*I'm a soldier.*
Congregation:	*In the army.*

It doesn't matter which phrase the leader sings ("I've got my war clothes on, I'll fight till I die, If I die, let me die") the congregation always responds the same. This just reiterates the fact that no matter what life throws at you, once you sign up to serve the Lord, you must respond with the same faith and trust in the Lord each time. Remember that it is the Lord you are serving, and you should respond to life as the Lord would have you to.

My sister told me about an incident in which she began to feel a little "road rage." When she told my mother what happened, my mother told her to look at the bracelet on her arm with the letters WWJD (What Would Jesus Do?) instead of retaliating. Even when life and those we love the most try to mock our service to God or make us question our commitment, we must continue to serve. This goes back to the question, "How may I serve you?"

Sometimes in our Christian walk, we do not follow the Lord even when he gives us specific instructions. Often we feel that he is not moving fast enough. If we are in front of the Lord trying to go places he has not prepared for us to go, we make many mistakes. We can think we are ready when we are not.

At the same time, if we are unwilling to take a step of faith and move out of our comfort zone, we will miss many blessings because we are not moving with the timing of the Lord. In Deuteronomy, after the Lord let Joshua know the soldiers could take the land, they still did not believe. They changed their mind when they saw God begin to move and decided that they would go up anyway. The problem with this was that God was not with them at that time. They had missed the timing of God and instead of getting the victory, they suffered a defeat. This incident underscores the need to not only move in the will of God but to understand the timing of God. That is the reason for the word of God being here for us. It is like the markings on a walking track. They are there to let you know how many times you need to go around the track in order to walk a mile. A mile is the same distance on any terrain, but treacherous terrain can make the mile seem longer. It also requires better equipment. You know the type of shoes you will need for that particular surface.

Sometimes in our walk, instead of following God, we want to follow what is popular or what the crowd is doing. That is whey we stumble around in our sin sometimes for years before we see the light of the Lord.

In the movie *Facing the Giants* a football team from a small high school had to take on a powerhouse team to win the state championship. They had played some tough teams to get there and the team they faced last was the toughest one. The coach admonished the team to stop looking at the record of the team they were facing. Just like Goliath, the Giants team was famous for making mincemeat out of all the teams they played. Teams that played them, especially smaller teams like the one the movie focused on, would end up trying to just get through the game uninjured instead of playing to win. However, the coach of this team had faith that they would make it and did not give up even when it looked like they were out of the championship after a playoff loss.

This happens to us sometimes in our lives. We look at the circumstances surrounding our situation and think we are outmatched. It is one thing to feel like it is just us against the world and we do not have a chance. It's a completely different situation to see us and God working together and believing that we can do all things through Christ.

In *Facing the Giants*, one man would just walk the halls and pray for the students on a regular basis. He prayed for the students, coaches and teachers. Many of them did not know him, but he prayed for them anyway. God used him as a prayer warrior to help change the lives of many of the students. He prayed that the students would be prepared for whatever circumstances they faced in life. Most of them never knew he prayed for them, but that didn't stop him. Likewise, we never know who God is using as our prayer warrior to get us where we need to be.

Anytime anyone tries to come against the army of God, they are defeated. Ephesians 6:12 lets us know that in our walk we are not fighting against flesh and blood. In other words, we are not fighting people. Our enemy is Satan. He is the one who does not want us to succeed. He is the one who wants to hinder us in our walk. He does not care how he goes about doing damage or who he uses to obtain his purpose as long as he is able to get our mind off God and onto something else.

Our responsibility is to use our own weapons of warfare that God has given us (Ephesians 6: 13-17) and to march on in this spiritual battle. We can be assured of our victory because Christ has already paid the ultimate price for us and already told us that we will win.

Many people who would like to have a regular exercise routine never begin because they fear the big picture (not being able to maintain an exercise regimen) rather than starting out and trusting the Lord to lead them to finish. We are reminded in Romans 12:3 that all are given a measure of faith; we just need to learn how to move at our own pace as God leads us.

In one exercise video, Leslie Sansone talks about the steps of a routine and emphasizes that participants can always modify the steps or routines to fit their current fitness level. Likewise, we just need to begin and keep moving. It does not matter if we cannot move as fast or as often as others as long as we are moving in the right direction with the Lord leading us.

All we need is the faith to begin the journey. We are all given a measure of faith. Our faith level may not be the same as the next person, but rest assured, it is enough to get us where we need to be until God increases our faith.

My own journey toward good spiritual health began much the same as my journey toward good physical health. I have always had a small to medium body frame and not much of a weight problem, so I never really thought about exercise or staying healthy. For the most part, I had always been pretty healthy. I was blessed with the metabolism to eat what I wanted and not gain weight. Then the age of thirty came.

Once I began to have some health concerns,

I became more conscious of taking better care of myself. I started exercising regularly and eating better, skipping seconds, eating smaller portions, cutting out most fried foods and eating salads and drinking more water. That worked well for a while. Because the true commitment was not there, I started and stopped several times. I would walk faithfully and watch what I ate. I would stay on a regular schedule of exercise for a while and then start to slack off just a little bit at a time until I was no longer exercising at all and was eating as much of everything I wanted. Of course, this period was followed by weight gain and feeling unhealthy. It took me a while, but I soon learned the importance of consistency and balance.

It also took me a while to reach the same level of commitment spiritually. Years ago, I would have been very comfortable saying that I have been serving and walking with the Lord most of my life. I had always considered myself a "good" Christian and saw no reason to make any adjustments in my life. I was happy. I believed I lived as good of a Christian life as I saw other people model. The fact that I did not have a true relationship with Christ was really not that big of a deal to me at the time. As a matter of fact, many people thought I was saved long before I actually made my profession of faith, so I figured I was doing pretty well.

I was concerned that my "public" walk always be presentable, unconcerned about having a true relationship with the Lord. That is until I heard a message one night that made a difference to me, convicted my spirit and forced me to face where I really was on this Christian walk. Of course, I have made mistakes and wandered off track a time or two, but my faith remains strong and the commitment to serve is still there. The following verse is inspirational to me during times of struggle: *I have no greater joy than to hear that my children walk in truth.* 3 John 4-6.

When the rich man asked Jesus what he needed to do to be saved (Matthew 19:18-24), he did not seem to be surprised when Jesus reminded him of what I call the basics of keeping the commandments. He told Jesus that he had kept the commandments since his youth and then asked what else? When Jesus told him, if he wanted to be perfect, to go sell all that he had and give it to the poor, the man went away sorrowfully because he was unwilling to part with his riches. He was willing to serve until he was asked to give up the one thing that he valued most. He was not willing to walk away from his wealth even to follow Jesus.

His response was very different from Saul's response when he was traveling on the road to Damascus: "And he trembling and astonished said, Lord, what will thou have me to do?" Acts 9:6a. Saul might very well have asked, Lord, how may I serve you? He did not ask God for a list of benefits he would receive if he followed him. He offered God complete trust without reservation.

Likewise, circumstances in our walk with the Lord are not supposed to change our desire to serve him. Job said, "though you slay me, yet will I trust you." This was after Satan believed that if God took the hedge from around him that he would turn his back on God.

As a servant of God, our main objective should be service to him. We all have the opportunity to walk with the Lord. Dr. Martin Luther King, Jr. once said,

Anybody can serve. You don't have to have a college degree to serve. You don't have to make your subject and your verb agree to serve. You don't have to know about Plato and Aristotle to serve. You don't have to know Einstein's theory of relativity to serve. You don't have to know the second theory of thermodynamics in physics to serve. You only need a heart full of grace. A soul generated by love.

Chapter 2
A Changed Walk

True repentance requires change. Once we begin our walk with the Lord, we must put our faith in him to lead us on the rest of our journey. We must act on that faith. As fitness expert Donna Richardson says in her "Sweating in the Spirit" workout, you have to want to change more than you want to stay the same.

I would often tell my children as they were growing up that good habits form the same way bad habits form. Consider this quote: "Watch your thoughts; they become words. Watch your words; they become actions. Watch your actions; they become habits. Watch your habits; they become your character. Watch your character; it becomes your destiny" (author unknown). If you are comfortable with the current habits you have, then you will have no desire to change. Usually, you will need some type of motivation to want to do something different.

It has been said that as soon as a person stops

smoking, the lungs begin to heal and as soon as someone stops drinking, liver damage decreases. As soon as we give our lives to Christ, we become a new creature (II Corinthians 5:17).

Change is not easy for a lot of people, even when it is necessary to reach a goal. The rich man who came to Jesus was sincere in his desire to have eternal life, but he was unwilling to make the one change necessary to move to the next level of commitment. Complacency can easily replace commitment when our desire to remain in our comfort zone is stronger than our desire to change.

Some people will serve until it calls for a change in their attitude or lifestyle. Others will serve until it calls for a sacrifice on their part, just like the rich man who went away sorrowfully after being told to sell what he had and give to the poor. In some churches, people who have already decided in their hearts that there is only so much that they are going to do. They will help in certain programs or in certain ways, but if a situation calls for something they are not willing to sacrifice, then their level of commitment ends.

Jesus gave us the example of how to serve.

He was God, but he was still humble enough to wash feet. He said, "I am among you as one who serves." How can we serve God without serving others?

Often in relationships, people would rather remain stagnant rather than put forth an effort to help the relationship grow and maintain a level of commitment past what they are willing to do. If they have been hurt, they will sometimes put up a wall of defense. They don't get hurt, but they also miss out on all the rewards of a truly committed relationship. Sometimes people are so focused on making sure the other person doesn't have the opportunity to hurt or disappoint them they take away that person's opportunity to truly love them.

People often cannot maintain their spiritual health because they are not willing to put time and effort into it. They make the same excuses they do for not exercising. They don't have the time or cannot afford a gym. However, there are solutions to that. We can do routines that require a little time and purchase of an inexpensive exercise video. Fitness videos and books are also available for free from local libraries.

The same principle is true with the desire for

a closer walk with the Lord. People don't feel they have time to work on their relationship with God. Just as they make excuses for not exercising, they make excuses for not putting time into maintaining a healthy walk with the Lord.

However, if something is important enough, we will make time for it. You can always start small and work you way up. Remember that faith the size of a mustard seed can move a mountain (Matthew 17:20).

A health instructor once told a class that instead of trying to lose weight, a better incentive is to stop gaining weight. Once we realize what is causing us to eat unhealthily or to resist exercise, we can remove those obstacles. Weight loss and healthy eating will naturally follow.

I once heard Paul White quote Bishop T. D. Jakes as saying, "you can't conquer what you won't confront, and you can't confront what you don't acknowledge." Again, there is not true repentance without change.

The woman caught in the act of adultery was brought before Jesus. The crime was punishable by stoning. Her accusers left when Jesus asked those without sin to cast the first stone. However, he did not leave it there. He told her he did not condemn her but for her to go and sin no more. Many times we forget about the last lesson in the story. We want to hear him say neither do I condemn, but we don't want to hear go and sin no more. We don't want to stop sinning. We don't want to change.

We want to walk in the grace of God without submitting to the will of God. Remember the question, shall we continue in sin so that grace may abound (Romans 6:1)? The answer is God forbid. Not just no, but God forbid. This is strong language for a serious question.

Unlike the woman at the well, we often want our walk to remain at the "neither do I condemn thee" stage. We want to be known as a Christian, but without putting forth any effort.

Often the first step toward spiritual health is to walk away from sin or other situations weighing us down. The Bible admonishes us in Hebrews 12:1 to lay aside every weight and sin that so easily besets us. However, some people need motivation to change. If someone is able to eat what they like and stay at a good weight, they can start to believe that they are healthy and don't need to exercise. Spiritually, we just become complacent and feel that if we are not doing anything really bad, that justifies the fact that we are not really "doing anything" at all.

As I mentioned earlier in describing my walk, it is easy to convince yourself that even if you are not walking a perfectly straight and narrow path, you are still doing fine. This is especially true when you measure your walk by your own standards and justify your sin as less than everybody else's.

Some people apologize for their actions when they mistreat or hurt someone but then do nothing to change the behavior that is hurtful or damaging to a situation. That makes it difficult for the person hurt to believe that those in the wrong truly want to change and makes them seem less than remorseful. Some people are truly apologetic for their wrongs and some people are sorry that they got caught. They have no remorse in their hearts and their agendas continue to be self-serving.

As with any change in your physical health, the desire to make a change to improve your spiritual health also must be greater than your desire to remain the same. It must be a continual process --

not just a quick fix. The children of Israel wandered around for years. They went from one situation to another seeming to forget how God delivered them from each one as soon as a new situation arrived. Yet, each time they got into trouble, they asked Moses to go to God for them.

Some people are reluctant to make any kind of commitment to change because they are afraid they can't stay committed. However, God has not given us a spirit of fear (2 Timothy 1:7). It is better to trust the Lord and seek his guidance in what commitments to make. Continue to trust him for the strength, courage and faith to keep those commitments. Walking with the Lord and keeping his commandments and doing his will make it easy to know which commitments to work toward and what to refuse.

God did not intend for us to try to walk this walk without his help. He is there for us at every turn. It is up to us to trust him to lead us and to be willing to follow his lead even when he leads us into areas we do not think we are equipped to go.

Many people fear or reject any kind of change. They cannot follow God because they fear relinquishing what they feel is control of their lives. This amazes me because (whether we accept it or not) God is in control. Our future lies in his hands. It does not matter how much we plan and prepare, the final outcome is in God's hands.

Our level of service often depends on our level of commitment. This applies to anything. How we exercise and see the need for exercise will also determine our benefit from physical fitness. We have often heard that some students would do a lot better in school if they would only apply themselves. Students who do fairly well without much effort are not motivated to give their best. They do just enough to get by. The down side of that is they put forth little effort, but they also gain little reward.

That's similar to my early Christian walk. I was not doing anything particularly bad. I was just not doing anything particularly good to insure my walk was where the Lord wanted it to be. I was just doing what was expected hoping for the best of what I could get from God, basically seeking the hand of God rather than the face of God. If we seek the face of God, we seek to know what we can do to get closer to God, to walk with him daily. We walk in his will because that's what we want to do instead of because that's what mama or grandmamma did back in the day.

Our attitude toward serving has a great deal to do with the type of service we will give to those we serve. If we see service to God as a dreaded obligation, the quality of our service will be sorely lacking or it will become a ritual rather than a way of life. It has to be about a way of life rather than a particular task. Remember you have to want to change more than you want to stay the same. Some people see salvation as the publicans and Pharisees saw it. This type of people literally serves the Lord "religiously," validating their service to God by the number of services they attend, rituals they perform, committees they serve on, etc. It stops being about the Lord and becomes about the "attention" or "praise' they receive for the amount of work they do.

Think about what you expect from a server in a restaurant. You expect to be served to your level of satisfaction. Many of us have had the "pleasure" of being served by someone whose attitude made it apparent from the minute they walked over to the table that they were in the wrong job. Their attitude toward service left a lot to be desired. Now compare that to service you received from someone who loved what they were doing and you knew would give you great service regardless of what you were able to leave them as a tip. Many servers will serve you a certain way depending on what they presume you will be able to leave them as a tip. At times we treat the Lord just like that. We think, "Lord, I will do as much as I am blessed". In other words, I am only going to do as much as it takes to get what I want at the time. If all servers want in a restaurant is the tip, then they will do whatever they can to get that tip. Are you treating God like a server in a restaurant? Is your service toward him dependent on what he gets you or how fast he can refill your "glass" in life with whatever you want to "drink"?

The movie *Fireproof* is the story of a couple who has grown apart and is heading toward divorce. The husband's father asked him to wait forty days before he started divorce proceedings and to use something that had helped him in his own marriage. After some consideration, he agreed, albeit begrudgingly, because he felt that his wife didn't deserve it. He did not understand the love of God at that point or the meaning of grace. He later came to understand that when we put more effort into something, we get more out of it. The old adage you get what you pay for has some merit. Sometimes we try to walk with God by trying to get by with as little effort as possible or far sitting back and letting others do all the work while we take all the credit. We want to reap the benefits without making any sacrifices or putting forth any effort. The Bible clearly lets us know in Luke 12:48 that to whom much is given, much is required.

In *Fireproof*, the husband's initial reluctance to change centered on the fact that he believed it wouldn't make a difference to his wife. He felt that if his wife was not willing to change some of her ways, then she didn't deserve for him to make the sacrifice of making changes in his own behavior. Likewise, she did not believe that he would continue in the changes he was making. She thought he was making the changes for the wrong reasons, which initially he was.

Sometimes, we choose how we will treat people or what we will give to people based on what it will cost us. Unfortunately, our service to God is sometimes based on how much sacrifice it requires on our part instead of what God has asked us to do. Satan does not mind taking advantage of the fact that sometimes being in difficult situations can cloud our judgment and our thinking, causing us to do things we would not otherwise do.

The interesting point about the movie *Fireproof* is that they both come to realize their own part in allowing the marriage to get to the point it was. They both had issues that they needed to deal with as well as past hurts they were having trouble forgiving each other for.

It took the wife a little longer to reach a deeper understanding in God also. The husband was trying to move to a deeper level with God and love his wife as God would have him to, the way Christ loved the church. His wife did not trust that he was really changing. Instead of trying to meet him half way, she started becoming friendlier with a doctor that she worked with. This doctor was giving her the attention that she longed for from her husband. This caused her to see the doctor through the eyes of her troubled marriage. She began to feel that the doctor was just a good man trying to help her feel better because she was in a bad situation. However, one of her friends brought up the fact if this doctor was such a good man, why was he trying to go after another man's wife? A "good" man would not do that. Remember, "The steps of a good man are ordered by the Lord." Psalms 37:23. Because she was dissatisfied with her husband, she did not see how self-serving this "good" doctor's motives were.

On the other hand, when her husband really began to put his heart into the project his father had asked him to complete, she had a change of heart. Early on as he tried to move the relationship to a deeper level, he ordered her some flowers based solely on the "cost," and he got what he paid for. He ended up with a pitiful looking bunch of flowers that did not impress his wife. Later on he ordered roses without regard to the cost. The first time he had chosen a price that he was willing to pay and accepted that whatever came for that price would be good enough because that was all he was willing to pay. By the time he ordered the second roses, he was at the point where he wanted to do something that would touch her heart no matter what the cost. It was no longer an obligation to him. It became a way of showing unconditional love. He had to learn how to continue in that love no matter how she responded.

Even after the husband walked through the difficult time in his marriage, he still had to work through some issues with his mother. He did not realize that he was harboring resentment towards his mother. He believed that he was doing not only what his father asked him to do in waiting forty days before filing divorce, but also that his father had done the same thing for his mother. He later came to understand that it had been his mother who had done those things for his father during a time when his father wanted to end the marriage.

We must learn in our Christian walk also. Sometimes we establish in our mind what we are willing to give up and expect God to tailor make our salvation according to the price we are willing to pay. It doesn't work like that.

Chapter 3
Walking in the Light

"Every man must decide whether he will walk in the light of altruism or the darkness of destructive selfishness. This is the judgment. Life's most persistent and urgent question is, what are you doing for others?"
　　　　　—Dr. Martin Luther King, Jr.

"Who among you that feareth the Lord, that obeyeth the voice of his servant, that walketh in darkness, and hath no light? Let him trust in the name of the Lord, and stay upon his God."
　　　　　--- Isaiah 50:10

I once heard Anne Graham Lotts talking about moths being drawn to a flame. She reflected that moth are not drawn to darkness, they are drawn to light. They don't have to be called, they are drawn. People who are lost will also be drawn to light and not darkness. Likewise, if you let your light shine, people will be drawn to Christ. It doesn't have to be a spectacular light. It can be a small light as long as the light is shining. You don't have to have a certain degree. You just have to let your light shine.

Think of a lighthouse. When you are in a distance, the light looks small from far off, but it has to be a powerful light to be able to be seen from miles away, and it is a guiding light for many ships. The closer we get to the source of the light, the better we are able to see just how bright it is.

The light of God in our life grows dim when we start to move away from God who is the source of our light our light and our salvation. My mother-in-law used to say, "When I see the light, I will walk in the light." You can be a long way away from a light, but if you see it, you can walk towards. If we are a city that sits on a hill, people need to see our light shining through our walk with the Lord.

In Ephesians 4:17-18, Paul lets us know that our changed walk is one that goes from darkness to light. In verse one; he admonished us to *"walk worthy of the vocation wherewith ye are called."*

17. This I say therefore, and testify in the Lord, that ye henceforth walk not as other Gentiles walk, in the vanity of their mind, 18. Having the understanding darkened, being alienated from the life of God through the ignorance that is in them, because of the blindness of their heart.

In the darkness, I believe that the real fear is the inability to access the light. If we know that we can turn on the lights when we need them, we don't fear sitting in the dark. That's because we are confident of the power source. The benefit of walking with the Lord is we do not have to trust in our own ability, but in the spirit of Christ that is within us. We begin to understand the power of the Holy Spirit evident in Philippians 4:13: "I can do all things through Christ which strengtheneth me".

Once when the power went off at our house, my daughter said, "We are out of light?" She was too young to realize that the lights need power to work. She just knew that there was suddenly no light. It doesn't matter if you have naked light bulbs or beautiful chandeliers all through your house; without a power source, you will still be in the dark.

The reason some people can't see our light shining is because we have left the source of our power (Jesus) and are trying to make a go of it on our own. Little by little we move away from God's will to our own will and pretty soon we have ourselves believing that whatever we want to do is God's will instead of the other way around. God did tell us that he would give us the desires of our heart, but that comes with the responsibility of delighting ourselves in the Lord, not in the desires.

The first lines in the song, "Amazing Grace" are "Amazing Grace how sweet the sound that saved a wretch like me. I once was lost, but now I'm found, was blind but now I see." This is not a literal statement but figuratively speaking. Lost equates with darkness and salvation with light. Once we truly understand what the grace of God means for us, we "see things" in a better light.

Anyone can serve and anyone can be a light for Christ in a world of darkness. Helen Keller once said, "It's a terrible thing to see and have no vision." So many times, we don't see what's going on around us. We follow the same path day after day and so much change happens slowly and subtly we don't even realize that we no longer recognize the life that we are living. There is a big difference in "looking" and "seeing."

When the soldier spied out the land and came back and said they saw giants, Joshua prayed, "Lord open their eyes." He knew they needed to believe with faith (that evidence of things not seen). Even though the giants were still there, their faith in God led them to believe that they could defeat them. Joshua was seeing the situation through the eyes of faith. Even though the soldiers doubted their ability, he knew that God would win the battle through them if they just allowed him to do it.

Often we don't see ourselves in the same light that others do. The song, "Too Close to the Mirror" contains these lines: "I'm too close to the mirror to see what you see. Why you shower down your blessing, your blessings on me. It's not anything I've done Lord as far as I can see. I think I'm just too close to the mirror to see what you see." It goes on to say, "you don't see me like I am you see me like I'm gonna be so I believe I'll run on and see what the ends gonna be."

So many times we fail to realize when we are going through trials and tribulations that it's not about us. It's about doing the will of God and serving him no matter what because that is the commitment we have made to him.

It doesn't matter how bad a situation appears, we need to hold on because we already know that if we wholly follow the Lord and allow him to order our steps, we will reign with him in the end. God has made the way so plain that even a fool could not err. We know that if we stay with God, then he will bring us out in the end if we continue to walk in his light (Psalms 26:1-3).

The light that people are looking for --- the light at the end of the tunnel -- should shine so bright through us that they know the light they need is Jesus.

When we profess to live for God and have the light of Jesus shining in our lives, people expect to see something different. Many people die daily and leave this world not knowing that they were loved or that they made a difference in somebody's life. How many times have we had an opportunity to share the light of Jesus with someone? Is there someone who could have been pulled back from the edge with a kind word or a smile or a word of thanks? Were you someone who dismissed a child of God who needed that "in as much" moment (Matthew 25:37-40)? Will God be able to look back over your life and see those things you did that made a difference? Or will you be reminded of all those times you could have made a difference and choose not to be bothered? We often don't realize that we cannot serve the Lord if we don't serve his people. In John 21:15-17 when Jesus asked Peter, loveth thou me? He responded to Peter's answer with, "Feed my sheep."

There is a song that asks, "If we are the body of Christ, why aren't his hands healing, why is his love not showing them there is a way?" There may be people lost today because they have not seen the light we profess to have shining in our lives. Or there may be many who have not believed in the light because our public and private lives do not shine with the same brightness. I heard say someone in a sermon once that people can't hear what we are saying because they see what we are doing.

Sometimes we are on the other side of the situation and spend our time watching humanity instead of God. We allow things that happen when people who step out of the will of God or even make honest mistakes, to hinder our own walk with the Lord. We end up focusing on their light instead of Jesus who is our main power source.

Walking uphill is hard. It takes more out of you because it requires more effort with usually less than satisfying results. So does walking in darkness while professing to live in the light. I'm reminded of a time when I heard a young person say that the only difference in the Christian is they go to church the next morning. I thought what a sad testimony for a Christian to have. I did not mean this judgmentally, just that if we are walking with God and the only difference the world sees in our lives is that we go to church and they don't, then we are not wholly following God. The fact remains that if our light is shining as a city that sits on a hill and cannot be hid, then the world should be able to see that light in our lives (Luke 8:16).

One songwriter wrote, "Let your light shine, shine, shine. Let your light shine, shine, shine.

There may be someone down in the valley trying to get home." If we are to be a city that sits on a hill, then we must be careful of our walk because people will justifiably interpret our call and commitment to serve the Lord by what they see in our lives. Jesus reminded his disciples that they would be known by the love that they have one to another (John 13:34-35).

After Jesus healed Blind Bartimaeus, he became a follower. After Paul saw the light, literally, he followed Christ with the same enthusiasm he had previously used to persecute Christian. I remember hearing a testimony of a man who had been addicted to drugs. He said that he was as serious about following the Lord as he had been about the drugs. That's a powerful statement. Many times people use the phrase "I saw the light" after they have had a change of heart or a revelation about something that had been hindering them for some time.

Paul and Bartimaeus behaved differently once they saw the light. Fitness expert Donna Richardson says in her "Sweating in the Spirit" workout that people have to want to change more than they want to stay the same. They have to want be free of the burden of unhealthy living and eating.

That principle reiterates the earlier mention of Hebrews 12:1 admonishing us to "lay aside every weight." Being weighted down with the burden of trying to conceal or hide sin makes our walk a lot harder. I remember an example that Paula White used of someone carrying a backpack that was very heavy. The walker began to take objects out of the backpack, it was easier to carry. We need to lay down all the ways of the world, and take up the cross of Jesus because his yoke is easy and his burden is light (Matthew 11:28-30).

You can fool yourself into thinking that you are on the right track and not be. Some people are not necessarily living in sin, but are not actually doing anything for the Lord either. Like I said earlier, people would assume that I was saved because I was in church all the time and not doing anything that appeared to be ungodly. However, I was only "acting" like I was saved, but I did not have a relationship with the Lord. I was fooling other people, fooling myself at times but certainly not fooling God. Some people may be in this situation and just not realize that being "good" is not the same thing as being "saved."

If you are able to eat what you like and stay at a good weight, you can start to believe that you are healthy and don't need to exercise. It's only when you start to pay attention to other things (tiring easily or becoming winded on a small flight of stairs) that you realize being thin and being healthy are not the same thing.

Bodily exercise is futile unless it's consistent. Consistency is also important in our walk with the Lord. Exercising your faith must be a way of life and not just a quick fix when you are in a pinch. This Christian walk is a life-long journey, and trying to walk it only when it is convenient or when it is self-serving is similar to self-medicating in the face of illness or pain that obviously needs medical attention. You can choose a lifetime of selfishly serving your own needs or a lifetime of service to others. It must be a lifestyle change. You have to want to change more than you want to stay the same.

The light that the world should see in our lives is Jesus. Often the light that people see is our own star that we put out in front for everybody to see. One songwriter wrote, "I don't wanna miss heaven shooting for the stars. Help me to keep my foot on the rock as I chase my dreams so far. If I ever leave your presence, I know I've gone too far. Don't let me miss heaven shooting for the stars." Sometimes we want to make ourselves the light instead of bearing witness to the light of Jesus. If we are not careful, we become captivated by what we think is our "own" greatness and our walk begins to take on that spirit of selfishness instead of the glory of God within us. This reminds me of the phrase, "You are a legend in your own mind."

Chapter 4
Maintaining the Walk

For bodily exercise profits a little, but godliness is profitable in all things, having promise of the life that now is and of that which is to come. I Tim. 4:8 NKJV

Many years ago, a gynecologist told me that what happens to a lot of women the age I was a the time is that they start gaining a pound or two each year and it doesn't seem like much at first because it's only a pound or so and they only think about it at check up time each year. But then they get on the scale a few years later, and they have gained ten pounds, and it is a big problem because they see the whole ten pounds. If they had taken care of the first few extra pounds in the beginning, they would not find themselves at a loss as to how they will lose the ten pounds.

Maintaining spiritual health is even more important. If you only think about your health in

January each year as you start another resolution to lose weight and to eat more healthily, you will soon fall back to your old habits of eating unhealthily and not exercising as much or not exercising at all. It has to be about lifestyle change, not simply to joining a fad or fitting into a certain outfit or being part of the latest fitness rage.

Maintaining a healthy weight will be easier if you consider how each meal or snack you eat will affect your body as well as your life. If you allow yourself to think about how you will face God after decisions and actions, it will be easier for you to make good decisions.

You must consistent in your health regiment once you reach your physical goal. Good spiritual health also requires daily maintenance. One joke states that some people don't realize they need to do the same thing to maintain a relationship as they do to start the relationship. If you stop exercising suddenly, you lose the benefits of your exercise. Health experts believe that you lose the benefits of exercise forty-eight hours after you exercise. Likewise, when you are trying to reach a spiritual goal, you must be consistent in order to maintain your walk with the Lord. You need to read and study his word daily and spend time with the Lord in a way to develop a good relationship.

If Christians slack off a little bit at a time in their dedication to this spiritual and physical walk, it probably will not hurt that much initially, but it can set them up to start going backwards a little bit at a time. Before they know it, instead of growing in their walk, they stagnate. There is a song called "Slow Fade." The words warn you to be careful of the things you do because things don't crumble in a day, it's a slow fade. Christians can allow bad influences to creep into their lives a little bit at a time and before they know it, they face irreparable harm.

Someone once said that you can't lead until you learn how to follow. If you follow the Lord, people should be able to depend on you to do what you say you are going to do because God expects you to honor your commitment. If God shows us that we need to do something, we must have faith that he is able to keep that commitment. Many times we put our faith in God for "almost" everything. We trust him for humanly impossible tasks and our faith never waivers. However, there are some little helps that we need to get through the day, and for some reason we feel like God cannot be bother for minor problems. Or rather, we forget about Proverbs 3:6 and don't allow him to help in certain areas.

When you want to track the distance you have walked in exercise, you can use a pedometer. The pedometer will tell you how many miles you have walked. It measures the distance by the number of steps you take. However, the pedometer has to be set to your height and weight and stride length to be accurate. If not, you end up with false readings and think that you are doing either better or worse than you actually are.

Likewise, you must follow Christ's example and maintain your commitment to God's word. You should measure your spiritual walk by your growth and maturation. We are all given a measure of faith. How we exercise that faith will determine how well we maintain our walk with the Lord and the quality of our relationship with him. If there is no evidence of spiritual growth, then your walk is stagnant.

We all know people who have treadmills in the garage with clothes hanging on them as well as people who have bibles they never read. They get excited about their Christianity in the beginning only to get lax and stop reading their bible or going to church or even spending time with the Lord after the initial excitement wears off.

You know what happens in a marriage if the commitment vanishes as soon as the honeymoon ends. The commitment to the marriage needs to be as strong as the original desire to marry was. I heard a pastor say that many marriages would be in better shape if the couple spent the same percentage of time maintaining the marriage as they do planning for the wedding.

Similarly, more people would derive a better benefit from continually exercising their faith with the same intensity to maintain their initial level of commitment. This should be a daily practice of building the relationship with God, constantly submitting yourself to God's will and not your own (I Cor. 15:31).

Just as the right equipment is necessary for physical exercise, we need to remain equipped spiritually to continue to be successful in our walk with the Lord.

The back of the vest that WalMart employees

wear only ask the question, "how may I serve you?" It does not go on to say "And if I serve you, what will you do for me. It stops right there with "How may I serve you?" In much the same way, Matthew 7:12 admonishes to do unto others as we would have them to do unto us. That's where Jesus stopped. He did not say that if they don't do right by you, then you have the right to do what you want to or whatever you feel is just punishment or retaliation. However, he did say that you will reap what you sow (Galatians 6:7).

When you first begin to walk or exercise, you won't necessarily see immediate results. But you have to believe that if you continue, you will gain a healthier lifestyle. Sometimes in our Christian walk, it is difficult to show people the love of Christ when we don't feel like we are getting any in return. This is especially difficult when the people who are not showing us love are the very people who profess to be followers of Christ.

I am often amazed at how often we think we can separate our walk of faith from our everyday lives. We believe that it doesn't matter how we treat others as long as we are good at the specific calling that God has placed on our lives. For instance, we think that if we are a good pastor then we don't have to be a good mother or a good spouse or if we are a good Sunday school teacher, then we don't have to be a good steward over God's blessings. We forget that as Christians, everything that we do in our daily lives reflects our walk with God.

The Bible asks, "How can two walk together unless they agree?" There is a quotation that says, If God said it, I believe. That settles it. I heard a minister respond to this once by saying that if God said it, it's settled whether you believe it or not. It's difficult if not impossible to follow someone you do not trust. If we trust the Lord to lead us, we must be willing to be committed to follow him and to walk worthy of the trust he places in us.

Sometimes the hardest thing for us to do is to change directions when we are going wrong or we see someone else going in the wrong direction. This is especially difficult for parents. Some people, including myself are directionally challenged. We have a hard time remembering how to get to certain places consistently. I can sympathize with other people who are directionally challenged because I have the same problem. I can't explain it and really don't understand how some people are blessed with a great sense of direction and others are not. I just know that it can be overwhelming at times. When you travel with someone who is unsympathetic to your situation, it makes it more difficult and even more overwhelming. It makes you more likely to make mistakes, which ends up frustrating you even more. However, when you travel with someone who is willing to help, it actually gives you more confidence. If we are walking with the Lord, we don't have to worry about him letting us go in the wrong direction, we just have to have to faith and courage to follow him even when he leads us in a direction we are not excited about going. Satan, on the other hand has no qualms about watching you take a wrong turn in life and will often put people in your lives to lead you astray.

There is a song that begins with the words, "she is running a hundred miles an hour in the wrong direction." This song may very well ask the question, if we are serving God, why is our fellow man not benefiting from that service? Just as it would be a terrible disservice for someone with a good sense of direction to refuse to help someone who is directionally challenged, it is just as bad to profess to serve God and not help each other. Often people do not feel loved because we neglect the small acts of kindness that we can do to show love to them. If we are the body of Christ, why aren't we showing love to those that need love?

Facing difficult circumstances in our lives can make us leery of continuing on our journey. But, we must continue to walk on. We have to believe that trusting in the Lord will transform our lives. If not, we will spend lot of time operating in fear instead of faith. Our focus shifts towards what might happen instead of remembering that God is there for us no matter what happens.

I am reminded of the time I was taking swimming lessons. I was afraid to practice jumping into the water even though it was only five-feet deep. I am five-feet seven and can easily stand up in five feet of water. At one point during the lessons, the instructor said, "I think I figured out what your problem is. You're still a little apprehensive of the water." That was his subtle way of reminded me that you can't learn how to swim if you're scared of the water.

Sometimes we are professing to have faith and are not making any strides in our servant walk because we are standing on the shore afraid to get our feet wet.

If we are going to lead others to Christ, we must first learn the way ourselves. Just as people who are directionally challenged need others to help them find their way, those who are lost in sin need the help of those who are saved to help them find their way.

Someone once said that we may be the only Bible that some people will ever read. That is why it's so important to live true to what we profess. Remember the quotation that it's often hard for people to hear what we are saying because they see what we are doing. If we are professing to live one way while actually living a different life outside of church, we make it difficult for people to see the true light of Christ in our lives.

My mother was sweeping up trash once and she said this is the way sin builds up in our lives. It starts with just a tiny little piece of trash or something dropped on the floor and left builds up and becomes a whole pile or an entire room that needs to be cleaned. We need to take care of problems or concerns in our lives as they come up. We can use the practice of "get thee behind me Satan" when he begins to try to hinder our walk with the Lord (Matthew 16:23). We cannot afford to wait until the path is completely blocked by our sin and we wonder how to get back to God. Sometimes we turn suddenly and look for God and can't find him because we can't see past our sin. Isaiah 59:2 reminds us that sin is what separates us from God.

The children of Israel spent forty years in the desert because of their sin of disobedience. It kept them wondering around instead of moving forward. Even though they had seen God work miracle after miracle for them, they still doubted his ability to get them to the Promise Land. They knew the mistakes of their forefathers, but they made the same ones. They would be initially faithful and obedient after God moved, but they were seemingly unable to maintain their faith in the face of challenges and spent many years literally walking in circles.

You can also become stagnant in your walk if

you get to a point where you believe you have "arrived." If you just come to church every Sunday and listen to the sermon and go home thinking you are where you need to be and anything that the pastor or speaker is talking about has to be for the other people in the church and not for you, you have missed the point of I Cor. 15:31 where Paul said, "I die daily." This suggests that our walk is a daily walk. The Lord's Prayer petitions God to give us this day our daily bread. When the children of Israel were in the wilderness, the Lord blessed them with manna from heaven daily. They had just enough to get them through that day and then the Lord blessed them again the next day.

In that same manner, we do not have to plan our entire faith walk when we first believe. We just need to continue the walk daily and trust God to get us through each day. That small amount of faith that we must exercise to begin the journey will offer enormous rewards. Matthew 17:20 lets us know the power of faith the size of a mustard seed. We can move mountains with just a little bit of faith. The only way to exercise your faith is to act on it. We do not need to comprehend the full movement of God with the first step; we just need to move as God leads.

We cannot allow our walk to become stagnant. We can end up in a walk of faith that does nothing for us or not as much for us because we want to let everyone else carry the burden of responsibility or sacrifice while we get the credit. On the contrary, we must continue to walk by faith and not by sight. Again, moving as God leads.

Our physical body needs movement to stay healthy. This is true especially after an injury. Physical therapy after an injury or a fall is just as important in the recovery as the medicine for pain. Often it is more important. Once my daughter fell from a slide on a playground and injured her arm. She did not break it, but she had to wear a sling for a while. She got used to keeping it held up in that sling position, close to her body even after she took the sling off. My mother noticed this and "suggested" (in a way that only grandmothers can) that she start relaxing her arm and stretching it out regularly so that it wouldn't be weak. She had held it in the sling for so long; she thought she couldn't straighten it out without it hurting. She was right.

It did hurt a little to straighten it out but once she start straightening it out, it became easier.

Likewise, if we want to grow in our faith, we

must exercise it. James lets us know that faith without works is dead (2:26). When we have been hurt, we have a tendency to hold our pain close instead of releasing it to the Lord. We just assume that's it better to remember the pain of past hurt instead of trusting God through the pain of healing.

A contemporary Christian artist, Steven Curtis Chapman wrote and recorded a song, *"Everything is yours."* In the song, he talked about what it was like to walk the streets of Nashville, Singapore, Manila and Shanghi. He saw people who are suffering from disease in Africa and reminded us that they too belong to God. The wealthy man and the beggar on the streets of Nashville both belong to God. When I heard his story of how he changed the last verse of the song after his young daughter was killed in an accident, it moved me to think of the amount of faith in God it took to continue in that. Sometimes the greatest accomplishments in our lives occur during the most difficult times.

The last verse of the song:

I've walked the valley of death's shadow
so dark and deep that I could barely
breathe. I've had to let go of more than
I can bear and I've questioned
everything that I believe. Still even here
in this great darkness a ray of hope
comes shining through and I'm
reminded that in life or in death, God
we belong to you. It's all yours Lord,
everything is yours....

As a servant of the Lord, we must walk in faith. We won't always be able to see with our natural eyes where God is leading us. But, we must have the courage to continue on our journey.

I heard someone say once that professing salvation and walking in sin is just like that because you are with a burden that's not yours to bear. It takes more out of you. That goes back to walking uphill or living saved without commitment.

In Deborah Bedford's novel, *A Rose by the Door*, I found this paragraph: "It's easier for us to be angry at God than it is for us to change ourselves. Faith is something different than you think it is, Bea.

Faith is not a passive resignation to life. Faith isn't fate. 'God will take care of my needs, but if he doesn't, I can't do a thing about it.' That's not faith. As a matter of fact, that's exactly the opposite of faith. Even when things seem their worst, you need to expect *all* of God's goodness and love your life, Bea."

Bea asked, "How can I expect all of it George, when I haven't seen *any* of it? " He responded with "Watch. Just watch." (p. 295-296).

> *For bodily exercise profits a little, but godliness is profitable in all things, having promise of the life that now is and of that which is to come. I Tim. 4:8 NKJV*

Sometimes one of the most difficult aspects of our Christian walk is finding a way to live a balanced life. I have heard some people refer to an overzealous Christian as being too heavenly minded to be any earthly good.

In Matthew 7:23, Jesus emphasizes that there will be "many" in the church who will minister in his name and believe they are his servants, while actually working toward the inevitable end to hear, "Depart from me, I never knew you." The Full Life Study Bible goes further to say, "To avoid self deceit, followers of Christ must be totally committed to the truth and the righteousness revealed in God's Word and not consider 'ministerial success' as a standard by which to judge their relationship with Christ." (p.

Romans 3:23 lets us know that we have all sinned and come short of the glory of God. I would submit that we have also all been on the wrong side of that thin line between faith and foolishness. God did say he would use the foolish of the world to confound the wise (I Corinthians 1:27), but I believe that if you are not careful, you can allow Satan to distract you in a way that you are walking in your own foolishness believing you are stepping out on faith. That is why it is so important to have that type of relationship with God where you hear his voice and follow his leading. This does not mean that you will not make a mistake, but you will be more willing to admit your mistakes, seek God's forgiveness and move on.

As the wife of a minster and lay member in

ministry for over twenty years, I have witnessed and experienced the disappointments that occur in a family when there is an imbalance in the lives of believers. There is a belief that the Christian walk is somehow separate from their walk with the Lord in their everyday lives. The earlier example of not being concerned with how we treat others as long as we are good at what God has called us to do also apply here. We often forget that as Christians, what we do or don't do everyday reflects where we are in our walk with God. Remember the example from the movie, *Fireproof.* The husband was an excellent firemen and he lived by the code of "never leave your partner" on the job. His friend admonished him once and asked how he could run into a burning building to save a stranger, but not show the same consideration for his marriage.

Those of us who are married to ministers might struggle with sharing our spouse's time, energy and resources with those whom God has placed them shepherd over, but that does not mean it is not possible to have a good balance and that you can't remain faithful and prayerful until that balance is achieved. God will even help you struggle through times when it seems that the balance will not come.

In Romans 14:17, we see that the kingdom of God is not meat and drink, but peace, joy in the Holy Ghost. If we serve God through righteous peace and joy in the Holy Ghost, then that accountability that we should have to our families and our Christian brothers and sisters shines brightly because everything is stemming form our walk with the Lord.

Exercising and eating right go together in healthy living. If we exercise on a regular basis without changing our eating habits, our exercise is not as beneficial. It is possible to walk or exercise in a way that does not burn enough calories to make a difference. Moderation and portion control in eating helps us to maintain a healthy balance.

Sometimes we avail ourselves of healthy portions of worldly things without balancing that with the word of God. We made time for everything except prayer and meditation. Some people can understand why it's important continually to work on weight, job or church to maintain a healthy relationship. We know what happens when we do not have home, health, or even life insurance and something happens. If the best health insurance is staying healthy, the best way to walk with the Lord is to stay in his will. There is a saying where there's a will, there's a way. I would take that one step further to say that God's will is always the best way.

I once heard someone say that God never promised us smooth seas on this Christian voyage, just a safe arrival. So many people spend their lives so focused on living in a way that avoids confrontation that they miss the valuable lessons learning from dealing with and overcoming adversity. They do not pay attention to things that need to be taken care of, hoping that if they ignore a problem it will go away.

People often refuse to acknowledge anger and hold the anger inside, and it manifests itself in other ways. Often they do not even realize what is going on. God did not say we should not be angry. He said to anger and sin not in Psalms 4:4. When you do not deal with or solve problems as they arrive, they escalate to bigger, unsolved problems. Unfortunately, it often creates a bigger problem than the initial one that could have been dealt with immediately with a lot less trouble.

Many times we clutter our walk working so that we will have something to do to take our mind off of our own personal responsibilities. Our goal seems to be to wind up at the end of life's journey, tired and worn out with nothing to show for it. It is admirable to work until the end; it is completely different to just work with no end in sight.

God expects us to work toward the goal of our high calling in Christ, but he expects us to follow his lead. It can be difficult sometimes to see that thin line that separates faith and foolishness (I Corinthians 1:27). Just make sure it is "God's will and not your own, because then you wind up with people seeing your foolishness and not God's grace and mercy. When you step out of God's will you are on your own. This is what happened in Joshua when the soldiers tried to go up on their own and fight a battle that God had already finished.

Trying to maintain a balanced walk can be like walking a tight rope. You are walking out on nothing but faith. You look around for those people who have told you they would always be there for you and find no one. Faith is even more essential at this time. In some venues, there may be a safety net below the tight rope or high wire. Perhaps the only net we have in this tightrope of life is the grace of God. Sometimes we lose our focus and we fall, and other times we get a little shaky, but we regain our momentum and keep going. If you are on a tightrope and lose your balance, it is a good thing to have a net there. Likewise, God is our net. He will catch us when we fall and we can get up and continue in the walk.

One important consideration in balancing our walk with the Lord is the realization that our life affects those around us, those who are accountable to us and those whom we are accountable to. Romans 14:7 reminds us that "None of us liveth unto himself and no man dieth to himself. Whether we live unto the Lord and whether we die we die unto the Lord, whether we live therefore or die we are the Lord's".

Sometimes we worry about giving an account of ourselves to others or others being held accountable to us, but not how we are doing in giving account of ourselves to God. While we are commanded to live peaceably with all men in Romans 12:18, we are also admonished to seek the kingdom of God first. Serving God should be our first priority. We should focus on those tasks that God would have us to do and walk as God would have us to walk. We will naturally be mindful of the people we are accountable to because that is what God has told us to do in his word. That's why it is important to find a good balance in our lives.

There can be a high price to pay for living an unbalanced life. You may have seen people working on a lot of tasks seemingly unable to complete or do a good job on any of them. They may get something done on a lot of different tasks or projects. But very few, if any of those tasks will be done well.

Though finding a balance can be hard, it is possible. As servants of God, it is our job to give, but we must also learn how to receive at the hands of those God has placed in our lives to give to us. Sometimes we are so focused on "it is better to give than receive" until we don't realize that sometimes we can block other people's blessings by not allowing them to "give into our lives" as God leads them.

Conclusion

*Ye shall walk after the Lord your God,
and fear him, and keep his
commandments and obey his voice, and
ye shall serve him, and cleave unto him.*

—Deuteronomy 13:4

*For all people will walk every one in
the name of his god, and we will walk
in the name of the Lord our God for
ever and ever.*

— Micah 4:5

How do you prepare your house for company? Do you prepare ahead of time, or do you run in right before they get there and toss everything aside or slide clothes, mail or other items you do not want seen into closets? A good hostess will plan ahead and be prepared.

Living your life ready for Jesus to return means being ready at all times. If you lived your life always ready for Jesus to come back, it is the same as keeping your house clean all the time. You may have to pick up something occasionally or move something to make more room, but you don't have to go through the entire cleaning process as soon as the company gets there.

If you are walking with the Lord and his spirit lets you know that you are doing something wrong, then you just make the adjustment and keep going. It's not a life-changing decision or move each time (although there will be times when that is called for). So, are you walking in a way that keeps your soul ready for Jesus to come back at any time?

It is possible that you may have time for a quick clean-up when unexpected company arrives, but when Jesus returns, there will be no time for a do-over. It will be too late. Those not ready will be left behind. Ask yourself if you are walking in a way that keeps your soul ready for Jesus to come back at any moment. If you cannot answer in the affirmative, then you need to make the necessary adjustments to clean up your temple.

Your physical body is God's temple. Present your body a living sacrifice.

Lay aside every weight that hinders your walk with the Lord. It is harder to walk carrying a load. My mother used to say laziness will kill you. She was referring to the tendency of some people (myself at times) who would rather carry heavy or cumbersome loads in order to take everything in one trip rather than divide the load and make two trips. They are able to get everything in one trip, but it is not a very comfortable trip and they often dropped or damaged what they are carried in the process.

I remember when the dean of my department at work was shredding papers and was not patient enough to follow the instructions regarding the maximum number of pages the shredder suggested. He figured he would save a lot of time shredding more pages at a time. He ended up having to spend the time he hoped to save and some extra time repairing the shredder when it jammed. It would have been better for him if he had stuck with the guidelines. He wasted a lot of time trying to take a shortcut. He ended up having to do it correctly in the end anyway. What's more, he damaged the machine and ended up having to buy a new shredder.

In Luke 5:5, when Jesus told the fishermen to launch out into the deep, they put their faith and confidence totally in him. They said we have toiled all night and taken nothing, "but nevertheless at thy word, we will let down the net." Sometimes we reach a place in our lives where we feel like we have toiled endlessly with no reward and end up right there with nothing for the rest of our lives because we stop short of the promise and don't launch out on the last step of faith to pull in that very treasure we have been fishing for all of our lives.

If we move when God says move, we will remain in his will. Sometimes we stop when we just need to slow down. Other times we trudge along mindlessly in a walk, refusing to acknowledge God as he tries to lead us in a different direction. Either way, we are not in the will of God and our walk is hindered. Serving God should not take us anywhere God would not have us to go.

We may not always be able to walk at the same pace as everyone else. The main objective is to keep moving. I have read that people can burn calories just by standing up. Isn't that amazing?

Perhaps the main point we need to understand and remember in walking with God is to walk "with" him. That does not mean walking ahead or behind him. Some people want to make public sacrifices and still not wholly follow the Lord in their everyday lives. The bible lets us know in I Samuel 15:22 that obedience is better than sacrifice. Many people have a problem with the word *obey*. They testify to obedience to God's word as long as it lines up with what they think are their plans or as long as they do not have to sacrifice something important. As long as God is allowing them to do what they want to do, they are happy and willing to serve. With that attitude, it's all about seeking the hand of God for what they want instead of asking him what they can do for him.

We have often read or heard about parents who work all their lives to make sure their children have everything they need or want and then never have a relationship with the child. They end up without the one thing that the children actually need more than all the stuff they are able to provide. It's easier for them to provide for the child materialistically than to work on maintaining a healthy relationship.

The majority of the book focuses on maintaining the walk. Some people start and stop a lot; more people have trouble maintaining that walk. Circumstances come up and take our focus off the walk. We begin to worry about the circumstances and neglect the details of the walk.

When we get used to a healthier lifestyle of exercising and eating healthier, our body becomes accustomed to that. We do what is necessary to maintain it because it becomes a part of who we are.

When I first started doing walk aerobics to a Leslie Sansone exercise video, I started with the first level along with a few of my friends working in the library. That was at least three years ago. Now it would be useless for me to do a beginner's exercise everyday. There would be no challenge and no resistance because my body is already used to a moderate amount of exercise.

When people grow in their walk with Christ, circumstances that would have gotten them off track as new Christians do not even give them pause because they have moved past trusting in their own strength and understanding to trusting in God.

If people can just remember where God brought them from, they can face any new challenge that may arise. When my oldest daughter went to college, she had chosen a sister school to the one I work. This was an economic benefit for us because her tuition would be covered. As the beginning of the semester approached, the school informed us that she would have to go on a waiting list for the tuition waiver. This would have placed an enormous strain on us financially and I did not know how we could afford tuition at a private school. I fretted about it at first and then I did what we as Christians sometimes do as a last resort instead of first. I prayed about it and left it in the hands of the Lord. God worked it out.

When my youngest daughter attended a different school and we heard from the school that she would have to go on a waiting list for the tuition waiver. I was already prepared. My first thought was "oh yeah, I've been here before. God, you worked it out then and I know you will work it out this time." And he did.

At times in our life when we hesitate to do what we know we need to do. We are so afraid of failing that we don't even try. It's easier to wish we could do something than it is to do it. We can continue to blame others for our inability to do something instead of trusting God enough to go ahead and do what he wants us to do. Remember faith without works is dead (James 2:26). Often we are unwilling to work to fulfill God's will, choosing instead to blame others and sometimes God himself. We have a responsibility ourselves and sometimes our dreams and desires are unfilled simply because we are unwilling to work hard enough to achieve them.

I remember once I was writing a play and kept putting it off because I was afraid it wouldn't turn out right. Of course, after much prayer, it turned out well. This book may have been finished a lot earlier if I had not fallen into the same trap again. There is also a novel that I have been writing for years and recently realized that this book needed to be finished first. I don't know the exact moment I realized this, but I do know that I have had time to have finished with it. The fault for not moving in

God's timing rests with me alone.

However, I know it is not too late. It's never too late as long as you are walking with God. It's never too late as long as we are walking with God and what he has promised is still stored up for us.

Health experts suggest that even people who begin to take better care of themselves later in life increase their chances of having a longer healthier life. Even people who have smoked a long time can start to heal their lungs as soon as they stop smoking.

Sometimes in life, we think it's too late to improve upon a bad situation or something we believe is hopeless. We begin to believe that something has gone on too long to be healed or a relationship has deteriorated past a point of restoration, but God can still heal and restore and there is no failure in God. God's time is not our time. God does not move on our behalf due to our impatience but rather by our faith. If faith of a mustard can move a mountain, how much more can we do with even greater faith?

The serenity prayer seeks God's guidance on peace to accept those things we cannot change, courage to change the things we can and most importantly, wisdom to know the difference. Some people spend a lifetime trying to change situations they have no control of while others end up destroying a relationship because they don't have the courage to change or to apologize. They are also unwilling to try again after they make a mistake. They lose their faith in God and in man without even realizing it.

Some people even go from a bad relationship to a better one, but end up destroying that good relationship because they are so used to the bad that they don't recognize the good for what it is and treat it as if it is bad. That is just another example of why it is important to find a balance in our lives.

An unhealthy balance occurs when parents spend all their time away from the children they love, trying to give them the material things they never had. We lose balance in a relationship where there is no give and take because one person does all the giving and the other person does all the taking.

The 80/20 rule has been used to describe the imbalance in relationships, organizations and churches. In organizations and churches some people believe that 20 percent of the people do 80 percent of the work. This definitely constitutes an imbalance.

The principles of the serenity prayer mentioned earlier become a lot easier when we allow God to give us the wisdom. We not only understand what we need to do to walk closer to God, but also how and when to share our faith with unbelievers as well as believers who have temporarily lost their way.

One of the hardest challenges in our own walk with the Lord is to watch someone who we know is heading in the wrong direction. They are unwilling to accept our counsel, and their walk will lead them places they do not want to go. The pastor in the novel, *A Rose by the Door*, had been praying for Bea and wanted to do everything he could to help. Unfortunately, we can only give counsel to people who are willing to listen and are open to receive them. It does not matter how much we love them or how much we want to protect them.

I remember seeing someone walking in a spirit of depression and dejection where it looked as if there was an actual physical weight pressing down on his shoulders. He seemed literally bent over from the weight of this emotional burden. God can lift those types of burdens for you when you walk with him. Jesus said in Matthew 11:30, "take my yoke upon you and learn of me, for my yoke is easy and my burden is light."

Don't make the mistake of trying to walk someone else's walk. At times we neglect our mission because it doesn't seem to fit into our plans, not realizing that God is trying to change our plans and get us on his walk and to follow his plan. We don't want to follow God's plan because we don't want to change.

Unless we are close to a situation when a person is going through, we only see the results of the walk not realizing what they have gone through to get those results. We see the results of their faith walk and can mistakenly think it has been an easy trip.

A good measure of our walk may be to ask the following questions. Are we leading people to Christ or teaching them to be followers of us? Will they find peace and joy in Christ or just disappointment in us? Are we saying and doing what is convenient in order to get what we want? Do we use God like a slot machine and keep pulling the prayer handle when we need something? What type of prayer life are you leading? Are we committed to walking with God or compromising with Satan? Can people count on us to keep our word or do they have to doubt your words or deeds? Are our yeas yea and our nays no? Are we showing God's *agape* to others or are we just interested in what we can get from them and then just tossing them aside after they are no longer of any use to us? Is this what Jesus would do?

Are we proactive or reactive in our walk with the Lord? Many people will react to life rather than live their life trying to make good choices when there is no major crisis or no one is watching.

In her book, *A Call into his Presence*, Evangelist Evelyn Johnson describes forty days of prayer. This paragraph from the fourteenth day of prayer shows a desire to offer sacrificial service without reservation, loving and serving God because of who he is rather than because of what he can do: We want to serve you God, behind closed doors where nobody is watching and we are travailing in prayer. Our flesh and our minds have been beaten down by this very life that we live. We want to serve you when nobody will tell us thank you. We want to serve you when things are not going our way. We want to serve you when there is nobody in the church. We want to serve you when there is no microphone to pray in! We want to serve you when there is no camera on us! We want to serve you God like Moses did so we can have a legacy and a testimony after our lives are over with the great signs and wonders which was wrought through our very lives because we yielded ourselves as servants to You, the true and living God. It cannot happen without a sacrifice!

I would like to conclude not with pat answers but with more questions. Can God trust you enough in your walk to hold to your integrity no matter what Satan brings to tempt you? Is your life an example of God-ordered steps or are you walking to the beat of your own drum? Take a look at your life and find out where you really are in your walk with the Lord.

> *The Lord redeemeth the soul of his servants; and none of them that trust in him shall be desolate. Psalms 34:22*